INVESTIGATING SPACE

The Planets

Anne Cohen
Photographs by Robert Pickett

Contents

A & C Black · London

Planets in the night sky

The Earth that we live on is just one of nine planets which are travelling round the Sun. If you know where to look, you can sometimes see some of the other planets in the night sky. They are so far away, they look like tiny, bright stars.

This is a photograph of Venus shining brightly in the early morning. Unlike the Sun and stars, planets do not give out light of their own. They look bright because the Sun is shining on them and some of the light is reflected back to us on Earth.

If you could see Venus close-up, it would look like this. Thick white clouds cover its surface and reflect sunlight very well. This makes it shine brightly in the night sky. From Earth, Venus looks like a tiny star, but really it is almost as big as the Earth.

Earth   Venus

Make a model Solar System

The Solar System is made up of the nine planets, their moons, the Sun and some very small, rocky bits and pieces. The planets travel round the Sun in almost-circular paths called orbits.

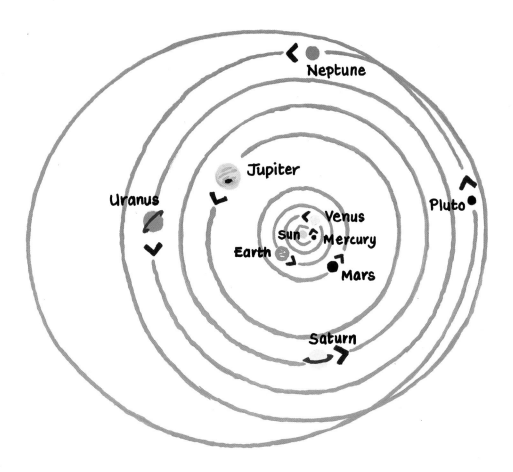

If you could look down from above the Earth's north pole, you would see that the planets travel round the Sun in an anti-clockwise direction. Pluto's orbit is tilted a little, and is not as circular as the others. Earth is the third planet out from the Sun.

To make a model of the Solar System to the correct scale, showing the planets' sizes and distances from each other, you'll need to go outside. But first you'll need to make models of the different-sized planets. If you use a beachball to represent the Sun, the planets will be these sizes:

You can make your models with modelling clay, or you can use things like table-tennis balls, marbles, ball-bearings and seeds to show the different sizes.

Now take the models you've made outdoors and space out your planets and Sun to the correct scale. You can measure the distances from the Sun in metre strides.

Mercury should be 12m from your beachball Sun.

Venus should be 23m away.

Earth should be 32m away.

Mars should be 49m away.

Jupiter should be 167m away.

Saturn should be 300m away.

Uranus should be about 600m away.

Neptune should be about 900m away.

Pluto does not move in a circular orbit. So in your model, Pluto's distance from the 'Sun' could be anywhere from 600m to 1.6 kilometres.

You probably won't have enough room for Uranus, Neptune and Pluto. See how much empty space there is in the Solar System.

Drawing an orbit

 Most of the planets travel round the Sun in paths that are almost circular. But Pluto and Mercury both move in an egg-shaped orbit called an ellipse. You can draw an ellipse using two pins in a board and a piece of string. Tie the string and loop it over the pins. As a pencil follows the string round, it will draw an ellipse.

If the drawing in this picture was of a planet's ellipse, the Sun would be at the position of one of the pins.

Day and night on Mercury

Mercury is the closest planet to the Sun and looks very like the Moon. Its surface is grey and rocky and covered with round dips called craters.

Mercury spins very slowly as it orbits the Sun. This means that one side of it spends a long time turned towards the Sun and then a long time turned away from it. During daylight, when sunshine is shining on the planet, the surface temperature can reach 430°C. This is hot enough to melt lead. At night, when Mercury has turned away from the Sun, the planet's surface temperature drops to −183°C.

Why is it so hot on Venus?

Venus is always covered in thick cloud, so the rocky surface of the planet cannot be seen. In 1991, the Magellan spacecraft made a map of Venus by sending radar down through the clouds which was then reflected off the surface. Magellan orbited above the cloud tops many times, making a bit more of the map each orbit.

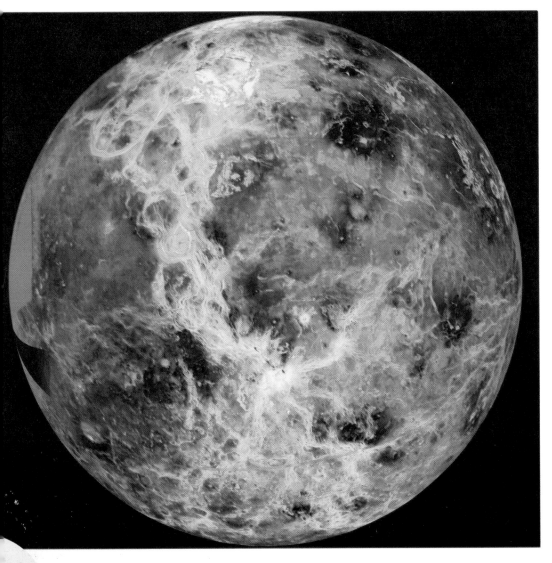

This is what we might see if Venus had no clouds to hide it. Nothing can live on the planet. The temperature on the surface of Venus is always 457°C.

It is so hot on Venus because the thick atmosphere traps the Sun's heat. This is called the 'greenhouse effect' because the glass in an ordinary greenhouse traps the Sun's light and heat in the same way. You can measure this warming effect for yourself by putting a glass-topped tank outside in the sunshine. After twenty minutes, measure the temperature inside and outside your 'greenhouse'. What do you notice?

Earth – the blue planet

Look at the photograph below of the Earth, which was taken from an Apollo spacecraft on its way to the Moon. You can see why the astronauts on board the Apollo spacecraft described Earth as 'the blue planet'.

The blue areas on the Earth's surface provide a clue as to why Earth is the only place in the Solar System which we know has living things on it. Earth is the only planet which has a plentiful supply of water in its seas, rivers and lakes. Plants and animals like those in this picture cannot survive without water.

The layer of air which surrounds the Earth is called the atmosphere. The atmosphere contains gases which protect us from the Sun's harmful rays, or radiation. (But we still need to protect our skin against sunburn when we are in the sun.) At the same time, the atmosphere lets the Sun's light and heat through to the Earth. Plants need warmth and light from the Sun in order to grow.

Most planets are orbited by balls of rock, ice and gases which are called moons. Only Venus and Mercury do not have any moons. You can often see Earth's Moon in the sky at night or early in the morning. This photograph was taken from our Moon, looking back at the Earth. To the left of the Earth is the command module of an Apollo spacecraft.

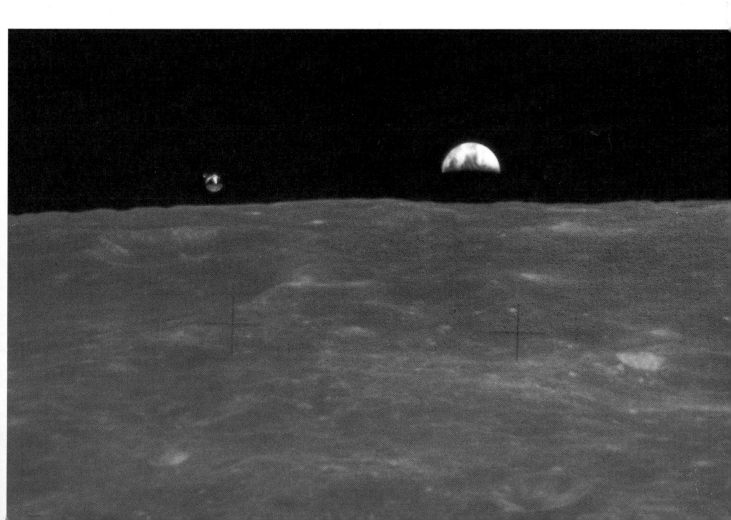

Mars – the red planet

The red rocks and dust on the surface of Mars make this planet look slightly orange if you see it in the night sky. The surface of the planet is a rocky desert strewn with boulders, and close-up we can see that it has many craters. These craters were formed when rocks from space crashed into the surface of Mars.

The sky on Mars is a pale orange colour. It is filled with red dust which is blown up into the air from the surface of the planet during wild dust storms. The photograph on the left was taken by the Viking 1 spacecraft, part of which you can see in the picture.

Mars has only a very thin atmosphere, which is mostly made up of carbon dioxide gas. It is so cold at night-time and in winter that all of the water and some of the carbon dioxide is always frozen. Mars has white ice-caps at its north and south poles. In the photograph below you can see the frost which speckles parts of the surface of Mars in winter.

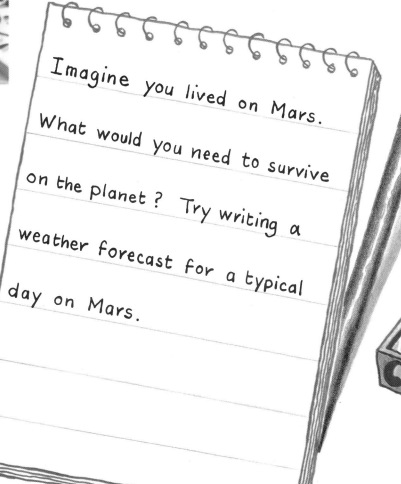

Imagine you lived on Mars. What would you need to survive on the planet? Try writing a weather forecast for a typical day on Mars.

Watching Jupiter

The giant planets, Jupiter, Saturn, Uranus and Neptune, are very different from the other planets of the Solar System. You could not stand on any of the giant planets because they are made mostly of gases and liquids.

In the night sky you can sometimes spot Jupiter. It looks like a very bright star. This is what Jupiter looks like close-up. Gases form bands of colour which swirl around as Jupiter turns. The Great Red Spot which you can see in this photograph is a huge whirlwind which has swirled for over 300 years. Two Earths would fit side-by-side across it. Jupiter itself is eleven times wider than Earth.

There are more than sixteen moons travelling round Jupiter. Many of these moons are very small. The four largest are each about the same size as Earth's Moon. Their names are Io, Europa, Ganymede and Callisto.

You can see these four moons if you look through a pair of binoculars. The moons look like tiny stars on each side of Jupiter's bright disc. Watch them change position slowly night by night as they orbit the planet.

Sometimes you'll only be able to see two or three of Jupiter's moons. Can you think why this is?

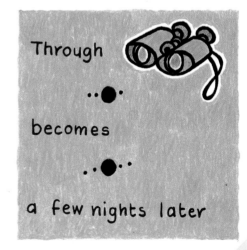

Through

becomes

a few nights later

Saturn – a gas planet

Saturn is not the only planet to have rings round it.
Jupiter, Uranus and Neptune all have smaller ring systems.
But Saturn's rings stretch out more than twice the width
of the planet. They can be seen from Earth through a
telescope. The rings are not solid. They are made up of
millions of pieces of rock and dust which all orbit Saturn.

Saturn is nearly all gas. Scientists think it may have a small rocky core at its centre, perhaps about the size of the Earth. Although Saturn is much larger and heavier than the Earth, the gas that it is made of is very light indeed. Saturn would float on water – if there was enough water to try this.

You can use a tank of water to investigate how objects made of different materials float or sink. Keep a record of the objects you used and the materials they are made from. What do you notice?

Uranus and Neptune in close-up

After the Voyager 2 spacecraft visited Jupiter and Saturn, it swept past Uranus in 1986 and Neptune in 1989. It took amazing new photographs of these very distant gas planets and their unusual moons.

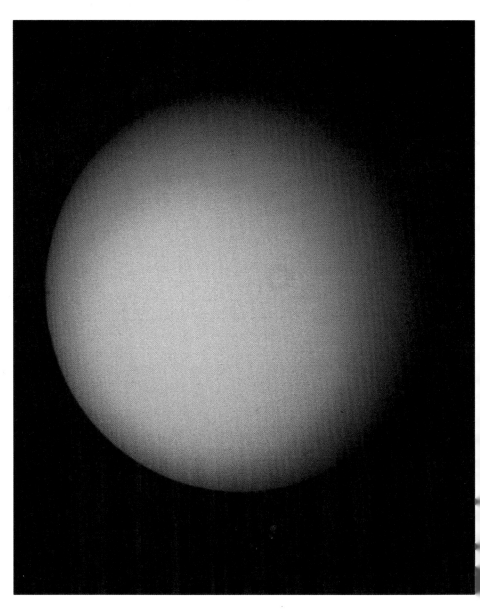

Uranus appears a pale blue colour with hardly any markings. This photograph shows the planet with its south pole in the centre of the picture.

Neptune's cloud tops are a beautiful deep blue. The bright, wispy white clouds which you can see in this picture are made from methane ice crystals. There is methane on Earth too, as natural gas.

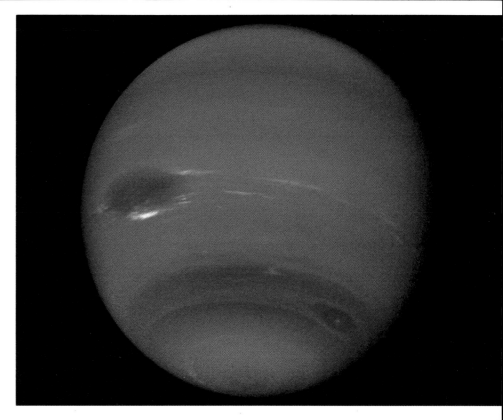

One of Neptune's moons, called Triton, is a pink colour. You can see Triton in the picture below. Triton is only slightly smaller than Earth's Moon. The temperature on Triton's surface is −230°C. This makes it the coldest-known place in the Solar System. Much of Triton is covered with ices and frost which look pink because of the chemicals in them.

As Voyager 2 passed Neptune, its radio messages were taking 4 hours to reach Earth. Imagine having a conversation with someone if you had to wait eight hours for each answer!

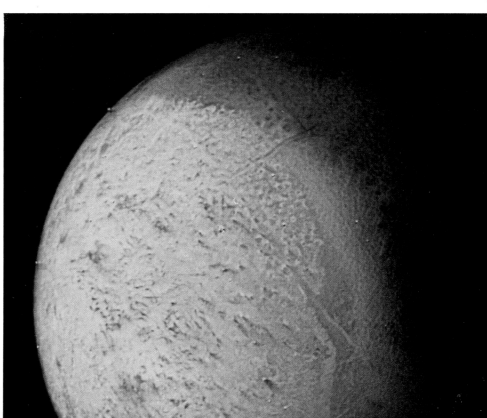

How was Pluto discovered?

Pluto, the ninth planet, is so far from the Earth and so faint
in the night sky, that it was not discovered until 1930. Clyde
Tombaugh, an American astronomer, searched through
thousands of photographs before he spotted a tiny dot which
had moved against the pattern of the background stars.
Planets orbit the Sun, so they change position in the sky
compared to the stars. So Tombaugh knew that the tiny,
moving dot had to be a planet.

Look at these two
photographs. The
'star' which has moved
is Pluto.

This is the clearest view we have of Pluto and its moon, Charon. Charon is about half the width of Pluto. Both are made of a mixture of rock and ice. The Voyager spacecraft's journeys didn't take them near to Pluto. This picture was taken through the Hubble Space Telescope which orbits the Earth above the atmosphere.

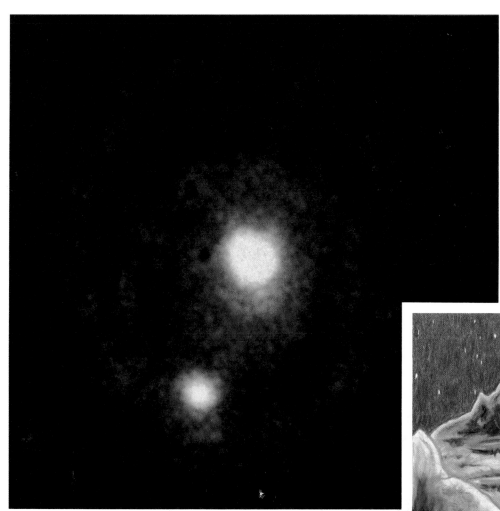

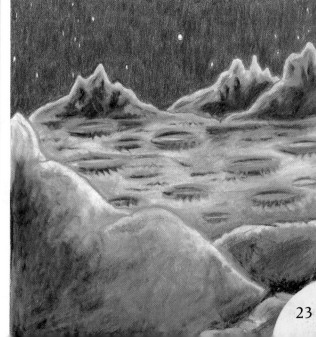

Pluto is the furthest planet from the Sun. From the surface of Pluto, the Sun would look like just another bright star in the sky.

Notes for teachers and parents

As you share this book with children, these notes will help you to get the most from the investigations.

Make a model Solar System (pages 4, 5, 6, 7)

The sizes and distances given here for the model planets are to the SAME scale. Many models use two different scaling factors, one for the planet sizes and another for the distances. While this gives a more convenient model, it conveys entirely the wrong impression about the distribution of matter in the Solar System. The model suggested here has planets which are large enough to handle, so it will need lots of space to spread it out correctly. However, the important point can be made without the outer planets, and you may need to stop at Jupiter or Saturn. Long strides will suffice for measuring metres. Remember that the planets rarely line up in a single line. To show this, the children can be encouraged to set off in different directions when they pace out the distances.

Large white or coloured cards showing the names of the planets can be carried by each person bearing a planet. This makes it easier to see which is which over the large distances!

Drawing an orbit (page 8)

You can extend the investigation by putting the two pins much closer together. This will make the ellipse almost circular. When the pins are placed on the same spot the ellipse becomes a circle. The length of the string can also be altered to make orbits further out from the Sun (i.e. further from the pins).

It is not only Pluto and Mercury which have non-circular orbits. The paths of some asteroids and comets are very elliptical.

Mars – the red planet (pages 14, 15)

A weather forecast for Mars should mention the temperature. At noon on the equator it can be a very pleasant 15°C, but falls to −80°C at night. The temperatures of the polar caps would also be very low, even in daytime, perhaps about −70°C. The atmosphere is mostly carbon dioxide. Thin, white, wispy clouds of ice crystals are sometimes seen. Great dust storms can rage for weeks, and can spread over the whole surface of the planet. This photograph shows the planet with its north pole at the bottom left-hand corner.

Watching Jupiter (pages 16, 17)

Even in street-lit areas, Jupiter is often bright enough to be seen in the night sky. To find out where and when to look, you can consult a newspaper, such as the weather section of the *Sunday Times*.

To detect Jupiter's moons you'll need good quality binoculars, e.g. size 10×50. It is hard to hold these steady in your hands, but you can rest them sideways against a door-frame or pole and this will help to keep them still. The binoculars will be even steadier if you mount them on a camera tripod – this also allows you to set up the binoculars pointing at Jupiter (or a star). Then ask the children to look. A special adaptor clip for the tripod can be obtained from camera shops for only a few pounds.

Most small telescopes will show Jupiter's moons well, but remember that the view is upside-down!

Saturn – a gas planet (pages 18, 19)

Objects denser than water sink. Overall, Saturn is less dense than water. Its density is estimated to be $0.7g/cm^3$ compared with water's $1.0g/cm^3$. This makes Saturn the only planet which would 'float', although it is one of the most massive planets in the Solar System. It is 95 times heavier than the Earth.

Uranus and Neptune in close-up
(pages 20, 21)

These two planets cannot be seen with the unaided eye, but can be detected using binoculars and a detailed star map. However, they don't look very impressive through binoculars – just like faint stars in the sky.

All the planets, except for Uranus, orbit round the Sun with their north and south poles in an almost vertical position. Uranus, however, lies on its side with its north and south poles along the plane of the Solar System. From Earth we only ever see its north or south pole.

How was Pluto discovered? (pages 22, 23)

As a puzzle, try photocopying the two pictures and blacking out the arrows. Can you find the star which has moved?

Index